A VISUAL JOURNEY THROUGH MANIA

How to Manage your Mania

Karen Stone

Copyright © 2022 Karen Stone

All rights reserved.

No part of this book may be reproduced in any manner without express written permission of the author except in instances of brief quotations in articles, reviews, and social media.

ISBN: 979-8-9859015-2-8

CONTENTS

Title Page
Copyright
Introduction
Symptoms of Hypomania — 1
Symptoms of Mania/Psychosis — 7
Suggestions for Friends or Family When Someone is Hypomanic/Manic — 13
Recommendations for Hospital Psychiatric Unit — 14
Appendix A — 15
Acknowledgement — 17
About The Author — 19

INTRODUCTION

This book was written with the goal of helping people with bipolar disorder manage their manic symptoms with a visual book. A second goal is to help people who live, or work, with people who have manic and/or psychotic episodes. There has been a lot of work, and help, for people with depression and anxiety, but much less information on how to manage hypomania (low mania), manic, and psychotic episodes.

I am not a bipolar expert in the traditional sense. I am an observant, and self-aware, person with bipolar disorder. This book is based on my personal experience of dealing with bipolar disorder over a period of 16 years. I have been hospitalized for mania and/or psychosis many times. I also attended a day treatment program for 9 hours a week, for one year. During the hospitalizations, I not only learned about myself, but I also met and observed other manic and psychotic patients. I learned the most when I became stable, and met newly arrived manic patients. I was able to understand them when other people couldn't, because of my personal experience with mania and psychosis.

There is a known scale for manic depression of 1-10:

Severely Depressed: 1
Depressed: 2-4
Hypomanic: 6-7.5
Mania/Psychosis: 8-10

SYMPTOMS OF HYPOMANIA

For any increasing symptoms of hypomania, calling or scheduling time with your psychiatrist, therapist, and/or case manager is important. If a clinician is not available, you can call your emergency contact, the crisis line, or 911.

The Key Symptoms of Hypomania:
- a. Irritabile/Argumentative
- b. Less Need for Sleep
- c. Impulsive/Risky Behavior
- d. Feeling Deliriously Happy
- e. Talking Too Fast (Pressured Speech)
- f. High Activity

1. Irritable/Argumentative

You have an inner belief that you are always right, and have difficulty listening to others. I kept a list of "good," and "bad," people, and these individuals quickly moved from "good" to "bad" if they disagreed with me in any way. I ended up with only two people left on my good side: my young daughter, and my sister-in-law who I only talked to on the phone. My bad list had about twenty people. The irritability, and non-stop arguing, can be damaging to relationships.

2. Less Need For Sleep

A decreased need for sleep typically means less than 6 hours for several days, and you feel wide awake. This has always been my first indication of hypomania, and it is the hardest to resist as it feels good to have extra energy. Try to remind yourself of the downsides of hypomania, like irritability and the risk of slipping into mania.

You need to increase sleep to 6+ hours. Try:

- Monitor sleep with a daily record (see Appendix A)
- Relaxation/Breathing techniques or listen to YouTube video
- Watch a movie or show you have seen before to relax
- Check with psychiatrist about medication to help stabilize your mood and help you sleep

Something to Consider:
Ask yourself: "Am I safe to drive a car?"

If you are not sure, don't drive. Instead you can ask a friend or a family member to drive, take public transit, or request an Uber. My rule of thumb is I don't drive unless I slept at least 6 hours the night before.

3. Impulsive Behavior

In a short amount of time, I bought a new car (Toyota Prius) off the lot. I rationalized it was okay, as it was an environmentally based purchase. Other impulsive behaviors include risky sex, excessive drinking/drugs. I have not had experience with these behaviors, but they may happen with hypomania (and mania) as well.

Preventive Measures to try:

1. Avoid going to stores when you are feeling

symptomatic.
2. Use only one credit card, and set an overall spending limit. Also, definitely set daily spending limits.
3. Learn return policies, and only shop at stores with at least 3-6 month return policies. Shop at stores that do not require a receipt.
4. If you are really drawn to certain stores, try to create a mental rule such as taking a picture of the item you would like to buy, instead of buying the item.
5. Only go to the store without a wallet. Bring a camera to take pictures of interesting things.
6. Let someone you trust take your computer so that you cannot shop on the Internet.

One of my goals was to not spend more than $100 in a given day, and I tried to only make purchases at stores with an endless return policy.

A Note: At one point my psychiatrist told me not to buy anything over $2. I thought, "I will only spend $2.00 in that store, and get a small item instead of a $30 book." I went into a Barnes & Noble in February, and found large "beautiful" calendars for only $2. I grabbed a bunch of calendars, and sat down on the floor. I picked out 24 calendars to give to relatives instead of Christmas cards. I was very happy with myself. The next day, I went to another Barnes and Noble, and put over 300 calendars in my cart. It was near closing time, and the manager was very angry. She said I would have to wait until the next day to purchase the items. I went back the next day, and bought the calendars. Then I started buying all the suggested books. A kind woman came up to me with an application, and told me about the employee discount. Needless to say, my psychiatrist was not happy, and shortly thereafter Barnes and Noble changed their return policy. They then went on my "bad" list.

4. Feeling Deliriously Happy

A VISUAL JOURNEY THROUGH MANIA

Feeling deliriously happy to me meant thinking, "everything is beautiful." It is okay to feel incredibly happy, it is just a matter of what you do with this feeling. This is not the time to try to brainstorm with your boss as I did. Instead, it is a good time to try your hand at art, journaling, or any safe creative outlet at home. It is another seductive part of hypomania that is difficult to resist, but again, try to remember the downsides of hypomania, and how it can turn into a very dangerous mania.

5. Talking Too Fast (Pressured Speech)

If you feel yourself talking too fast, try to take a breath and listen. If someone comments on your rapid speech, or says that you are interrupting, try to recognize it as help instead of getting angry. Be aware of your speech, and who you are talking to.

5

Especially if it is your boss or your children as there may be more consequences with them for saying too much. Try journaling to get your thoughts out. I finally realized something was actually wrong with me when a friend said that I was talking very rapidly. I finally slowed down enough so she could understand what I was saying.

During one hospitalization, I met two very manic patients. No one could understand them. One yelled and swore very rapidly, and people hated her. The other patient mumbled under his breath very quickly. At first, I couldn't understand more than a word here and there. After focusing for a day, and then realizing I was making an effort, they started to constantly talk to me. I began to understand them even though they could not understand each other.

6. High Activity

I wear a Fitbit as it is recommended to walk 10k steps per day. For myself, if I find that I am measuring 12k+ steps, without any intentional walking or exercise, it is a sign of hypomania. When I am hypomanic, I find myself pacing or cleaning in the middle of the night. When I finally relax, I sometimes notice that my feet and back are sore. It is best to try to slow down.

Ways to Slow Down:
- Take a bath
- Journal
- Draw, or do a form of engaging art
- Sit through a 30 minute show (I need the show to be new or engaging)

SYMPTOMS OF MANIA/ PSYCHOSIS

It is a subjective matter when a person moves from hypomania to mania/psychosis. On the scale, it is moving from 7 to 7.5 - 10. Different professionals have given me different scales to measure mania and psychosis, and it has always made it easier when looking back. Some clinicians said being in the mania/psychosis zone is when you need to consider hospitalization, but all agree you need to at least see, or call, your psychiatrist as soon as possible. Looking back, this is when I had memory lapses and my decision-making went downhill. I had to go into the hospital because I quickly spiraled to a place where I was a danger to myself, which is not always the case. The problem is, you get to a place where you are no longer self-aware and you can't make rational decisions. You need to go to a safe environment before your ability to make rational decisions disappears. You need to become very self-aware on a regular basis, so that you can catch yourself when you are still hypomanic.

There is still a chance you can catch yourself when you are manic, but it may have to be that a friend or family member has to help by hospitalizing you. I have gotten to the point where I am now aware of my visual distortions, delusions, and hallucinations, but in the past a family member sometimes needed to call 911 for an ambulance. The first time a family member did this to me, I did not think I would ever forgive them. However, going to the hospital is far better than ending up in jail, broke, homeless, or dead. I have not reached the point where I am manic, and am able to avoid a hospitalization. The hospitalizations are typically much shorter when you are voluntary.

In mania/psychosis there is an in increase in:

- Irritability/Argumentative (One hospitalization, the doctor said, "You take my head off every single day.")
- Sleeping 0-4 hours a day
- Impulsivity
- Euphoria
- Talking so fast that you are incomprehensible, and become frustrated that people aren't talking to you

In addition, mania/psychosis results in:

    a. Visual Distortion/Waves
    b. Distractibility
    c. Unable To Do Simple Tasks
    d. Unable To Manage Medications
    e. Paranoia
    f. Delusions
    g. Hallucinations

1. Visual Distortion/Waves

This to me, is a clear sign of psychosis. When I was in psychosis and I was looking at a Monet painting, it seemed like the water and the boats were moving. I was aware that this was probably a symptom of psychosis.

2. Distractibility

For one voluntary hospitalization, I asked someone for a ride, and I drove to his house. He didn't come outside when I arrived so I honked, became impatient, and then drove myself to the hospital. It was raining and I started to become mesmerized by the raindrops on the windshield. I kept swerving, and told myself over, and over, to "focus," but it was very difficult. I barely made it to the hospital without having an accident.

Another Example of Distractibility: Getting Lost

I used to work as a human factors engineer(study of human interfaces with everyday things such as computers, doorknobs, and stoves to make them easier to work with). In human factors, you try to design for the worst case, i.e. you don't design a sign for someone with perfect vision, but rather for someone with poor vision. I realized that when I was manic and having visual distortions, I was a worse case scenario for human factors. At one point, I stayed in a very old classic hotel near the Mayo Clinic, and I constantly became lost. The carpet mesmerized me, and I couldn't "see" the room number. I had to keep going down to the lobby, and luckily a kind bellman showed me to my room again, and again. He finally called a taxi to bring me to the hospital. I don't think I even realized what was going on.

3. Unable To Do Simple Tasks

I could not think what to do when the phone rang. I just looked at it and finally picked it up. Next, I didn't remember what to say when I answered. So instead, I just waited and the other person finally said "hello" and asked why I didn't say hello. I asked why they didn't say hello and it was quite comical.

4. Unable To Manage Medications

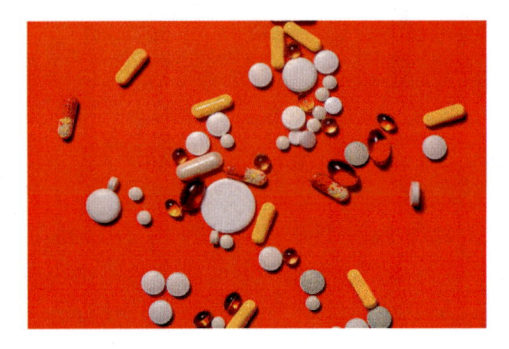

If you are experiencing mania or psychosis, or both, ask for help with your medications. A case manager, or the county you live in, may be able to send a nurse to help set up your medications. Another option besides the hospital is a crisis center where there are typically nurses and a psychiatrist that can help you manage your medication. If your medications become disorganized, this will only increase your chance of spiraling out of control and ending up in the hospital. Or worse.

5. Paranoia

As I become manic, I become increasingly paranoid. I remember being in the hospital and feeling like someone was following me. I would look back and see glimpses of a shadow, but could never see who it was. Most likely no one was there. If you are having severe paranoia, contact your psychiatrist quickly.

6. Delusions

If you are having significant delusions, you need to at least contact your psychiatrist. Delusions can become dangerous very quickly. At one point, after I had been watching a science fiction show, I thought that my family had been killed on 9/11 (not true). I also believed that I could travel between heaven and earth. I wanted to see my family, and believed I would have to commit suicide to see them. My daughter came home to see me sitting on the floor with pills all over, and she had to call an ambulance.

I was very surprised that recently when I had a delusion, I realized for the first time that it might actually be a delusion. I was in a hotel room watching T.V., and it seemed like every program (including an HBO movie, Dharma & Greg, and CNN News) was about some sort of mental illness. I suddenly felt like the T.V., or God, was trying to communicate a message to me. Then I thought, "this is not a rational thought." I called my dad to get a second opinion, and even though I could not let go of the thought, he helped me confirm it was not rational. I called my psychiatrist and he increased my antipsychotic medication.

As someone with bipolar or schizophrenia, try to stay self-aware and logical. If something doesn't make sense, ask someone else about it.

7. Hallucinations

When I have had a hallucination, it was usually a glimpse of someone behind me. My psychiatrist tells me to double check the locks, and check the rooms to validate no one is in the house. These hallucinations always correlated with significant sleep deprivation (4-8 days with 0-2 hours of sleep). Even if the hallucination doesn't last long, it is important to let your doctor know about it. There are specific medications to help with both hallucinations and sleep.

SUGGESTIONS FOR FRIENDS OR FAMILY WHEN SOMEONE IS HYPOMANIC/MANIC

1. The goal should be to help us slow down or de-escalate.
2. Don't try to argue with someone who is manic, it will just make things worse. I believed I was always right. (Exceptions are: safety issues like driving cars, or other dangerous behaviors. Sometimes calling 911 is the only option.)
3. Distract, distract, distract your loved one with safe activities like walking, art, games, or just listening (even though it may be annoying, remember their mind is racing. It sometimes felt like I had consumed 10 cups of coffee.) Distraction may work to remove someone from a store, but it may not. In the end, they are an adult. If they are not a danger to themselves or others, there is nothing you can legally do to stop them.
4. Help with structure and the basics: sleep, medication, and food. etc.
5. You can try relaxation techniques, but don't get discouraged. Try to put yourself in the patient's shoes. Think how you would feel if you tried relaxing after having little to no sleep and drinking 10 cups of coffee.

RECOMMENDATIONS FOR HOSPITAL PSYCHIATRIC UNIT

Get a recommendation from a friend who has bipolar disorder or schizophrenia, and who has been hospitalized before. When I was hospitalized and had to go to court, we picked up patients from different hospitals. I asked them all what they thought of their hospitals.

APPENDIX A

Daily Record

Daily Record	Sun	Mon	Tue	Wed	Thu	Fri	Sat
Take Meds							
Sleep (hours)							
Mood Scale (1-10)							
Anxiety Level (0-10)							

Mood Scale:

Severely Depressed - 1
Depressed 2-4
Hypomanic 6-7.5
Mania/Psychosis 8-10

Anxiety Level:

Not anxious at all - 0
Debilitating panic attack - 10

ACKNOWLEDGEMENT

I would like to acknowledge the hard work of Jane Gallaher, Kristen Stone, Wendy Gallaher, Lana Trendov, and my husband.

ABOUT THE AUTHOR

Karen Stone

Karen Stone is a brilliant woman and a loving mother, wife, daughter, and sister. She has a master's degree in biomedical engineering and worked in the field for twenty years. She has volunteered many hours in areas including mental health. Karen has been hospitalized over a dozen times for mania/psychosis and learned many things from the experience. She enjoys spending time with her loved ones, her dog, and learning more about the world every day.

Made in United States
Orlando, FL
24 August 2023